Symbols, Landmarks, and Monuments

The
Smithsonian
Institution

Tamara L. Britton
ABDO Publishing Company

visit us at
www.abdopub.com

Published by ABDO Publishing Company, 4940 Viking Drive, Edina, Minnesota 55435.
Copyright © 2004 by Abdo Consulting Group, Inc. International copyrights reserved in
all countries. No part of this book may be reproduced in any form without written
permission from the publisher.

Printed in the United States.

Cover Photo: Corbis
Interior Photos: AP/Wide World pp. 19, 25; Corbis pp. 1, 5, 6-7, 8, 9, 12, 15, 17, 18, 20,
    21, 25, 27, 29, 31; Getty Images pp. 24, 28; National Park Service p. 23;
    Smithsonian Institution Archives, Record Unit 95, Box 21, folder 7A, Negative #
    82-3196 p. 10; Smithsonian Institution Archives, Record Unit 95, Box 21, folder 9,
    Negative # 82-12239 p. 11; Smithsonian Institution, NNC, Douglas Mudd p. 13

Series Coordinator: Kristin Van Cleaf
Editors: Kate A. Conley, Stephanie Hedlund
Art Direction & Maps: Neil Klinepier

Library of Congress Cataloging-in-Publication Data

Britton, Tamara L., 1963-
    The Smithsonian Institution / Tamara L. Britton.
        p. cm. -- (Symbols, landmarks, and monuments)
    Includes index.
    Summary: An introduction to the history and museums of the Smithsonian
    Institution in Washington, D.C.
    ISBN 1-59197-521-2
    1. Smithsonian Institution--Juvenile literature. [1. Smithsonian Institution.
    2. Museums.] I. Title.

Q11.B895 2004
069'.09753--dc22

                                                            2003062771

Contents

The Smithsonian

In 1835, the United States received a generous gift. English scientist James Smithson had left the country a large sum of money in his will. He said it was to be used "for the increase and **diffusion** of knowledge among men."

The U.S. government had to decide what Smithson's purpose was. After much discussion, government leaders created the Smithsonian Institution. It had its own building and a board to run it. Many men took charge of the institution and made it what it is today.

Much of the Smithsonian Institution now stands on the National Mall in Washington, D.C. It has grown from one research building to many buildings devoted to art, history, and science. It is a symbol of a nation's support of knowledge and education.

The Smithsonian Castle in Washington, D.C.

Fast Facts

√ Today, visitors can see the crypt that holds James Smithson's remains.

√ The Smithsonian Institution's museums also provide traveling and online exhibits.

√ At the National Museum of American History, Behring Center, visitors can send a message by telegraph, pedal a high-wheel bicycle, and participate in many other historical activities.

√ The Smithsonian libraries hold 1.5 million volumes. They include 40,000 rare books, 2,000 manuscripts, and 180,000 pieces of microfilm and microfiche.

√ The National Museum of American History, Behring Center, is home to the First Ladies Exhibition. It features a selection of gowns worn by first ladies at presidential inaugural balls in the twentieth century.

√ The National Museum of American History, Behring Center, is home to the original Star-Spangled Banner. This flag inspired Francis Scott Key to write "The Star-Spangled Banner," the United States's national anthem.

√ In December 2003, the National Air and Space Museum opened the Steven F. Udvar-Hazy Center near Dulles Airport in Washington, D.C. The new center is so large that the National Air and Space Museum could fit inside it!

√ The Smithsonian is building a new museum called the National Museum of the American Indian on the National Mall. It should be completed by the fall of 2004.

Timeline

1829 √ James Smithson died on June 27, leaving his estate to his nephew, Henry James Hungerford.

1835 √ Hungerford died childless, so the money went to the United States.

1836 √ President Andrew Jackson signed a bill accepting Smithson's gift.

1838 √ Richard Rush returned from England with Smithson's money.

1846 √ The Smithsonian Institution was created; Joseph Henry was chosen as the first secretary.

1850 √ Henry hired Spencer Baird as his assistant.

1855 √ The Castle was completed.

1878 √ Henry died on May 13, and Baird took over as secretary.

1900s √ Supervised by various secretaries the Smithsonian grew, adding more museums and research facilities.

1996 √ The Smithsonian celebrated its 150th anniversary.

James Smithson

James Lewis Macie was born in Paris, France, in 1765. His father, Hugh Smithson, was the first Duke of Northumberland. His mother, Elizabeth Keate Hungerford Macie, was related to King Henry VII of England. James lived in England with his mother. His parents were not married. So, James could not claim relation to the royal family. Nor could he inherit his father's name or titles.

James's career choices were limited by this as well. He could not join the army, work in civil service, or join the church. So when James was 17 years old, he started classes at Pembroke College in Oxford, England.

James Smithson

James earned a master's degree from Pembroke in 1786. He became a scientist and a member of the Royal Society of London. James conducted scientific research and published papers explaining his results.

James inherited his mother's money when she died in 1800. He then changed his name to that of his father and became James Smithson. But, James still felt the limitations of his birth were unfair. If he couldn't be nobility, he at least wanted his name to be remembered.

Smithson often conducted research on minerals. The mineral smithsonite was later named after him.

The Gift

James Smithson died on June 27, 1829, in Genoa, Italy. He had not married and had no children. Smithson's will said his nephew, Henry James Hungerford, should receive his estate. But if Hungerford were to die before having children, the money would go to the United States.

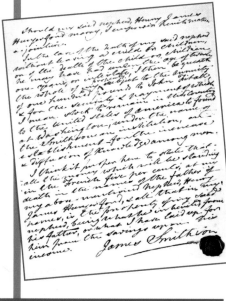

The last page of James Smithson's will, in his own handwriting

Six years later, Hungerford died childless. So, Smithson's $508,318 estate was given to the United States. It was to be used to build a place that Smithson called the Smithsonian Institution.

Most people would have been thrilled with such a gift. But U.S. president Andrew Jackson did not think he had the authority to accept it. He believed Congress would need to pass a law to make it legal. The congressmen **debated** what they should do.

Representative John C. Calhoun said the government did not have the right to accept the money. Senator William Preston felt it would be **unconstitutional** to accept it. Some congressmen felt Smithson was trying to make himself famous. After all, he had never even been to the United States.

James Smithson's grave in Italy

Finally, Congress decided to accept the gift. On July 1, 1836, President Jackson signed a bill accepting Smithson's money. Richard Rush, a diplomat and lawyer, traveled to London, England, to receive it. He returned with the gold coins two years later.

Congress loaned the money to several states. But Representative John Quincy Adams recognized the gift's great potential. He worked to get the money back. Finally, on August 10, 1846, President James K. Polk signed the bill that created the Smithsonian Institution.

John Quincy Adams

This is the back of one of the original gold coins Richard Rush brought from England. Only two of the coins survived. The rest were melted down and remade into U.S. money.

The Castle

Now the Smithsonian needed a home. The bill creating the institution said the building should be "of plain and **durable** materials and structure, without unnecessary ornament." Thirteen **architects** submitted designs for a building.

On November 30, 1846, **regents** chose James Renwick Jr.'s design. Renwick was a well-known architect. He had designed the Grace Church in New York. Later he would design Saint Patrick's Cathedral. His design best matched what the regents were looking for.

Renwick's design was for an **asymmetrical** building with **cloisters**, turrets, and towers. Inside, it included space for an art gallery, science museums, a lecture hall, a library, a chemical lab, and a natural history lab. People called the red sandstone building the Castle. It was completed in 1855.

People & Purpose

Next it was time to develop the institution itself. But this would be harder than it sounded. This was because people still **debated** what Smithson had wanted the institution to be.

Smithson's will said the money was "for the increase and **diffusion** of knowledge among men." Did that mean the Smithsonian should be a library? Or perhaps a school, or a lecture hall? Many agreed that since Smithson was a scientist, the institution should support scientific research.

The Smithsonian would be run by a Board of **Regents**. The board included the vice president of the United States and the chief justice of the Supreme Court. Three senators, three congresspeople, and six private citizens also sat on it. Today, three additional citizens are on this board.

The regents were to choose a secretary to direct the Smithsonian. The institution would support scientific research, so they decided on a scientist. In 1846, the board chose Joseph Henry as the Smithsonian's first secretary.

Henry was a physics professor at the College of New Jersey, which is now Princeton University. He thought Smithson's directions meant that the institution should promote scientific research. For this reason, Henry began a program of national **meteorology** research.

Joseph Henry's weather experiments helped lead to the creation of the National Weather Service, which tracks weather across North America.

Gathering Knowledge

Henry published the results of the Smithsonian's research. He also set up a way to share knowledge and research with scientists in other countries. But, all of this was hard work. Henry needed help. In 1850, he hired Spencer Baird to assist him at the Smithsonian.

Baird had studied at Dickinson College and was now a professor there. He had grown up in Reading, Pennsylvania. As a boy, Baird had often taken long walks and collected natural **specimens**. He soon had hundreds of examples of animal and plant species.

Baird's plan for the Smithsonian was different from Henry's. Baird felt it should be a museum. Henry did not agree. However, he allowed Baird to send out explorers to collect natural specimens.

Baird arrived to work at the Smithsonian in 1850. He brought two railroad boxcars full of natural history specimens with him.

Baird's ideas were the start of the Smithsonian's large natural history collection.

Lieutenant Commander Charles Wilkes and the U.S. Exploring Expedition set out into areas such as the unexplored American West. In 1858, the Smithsonian received items such as rocks, plants, animals, and Native American artifacts.

Baird organized the samples and soon had a large collection. Henry eventually agreed to a museum, as long as Smithson's money was not used to pay for it. In 1878, Congress gave responsibility for the United States National Museum to the Smithsonian Institution.

The museum opened three years later. It is now the Arts and Industries Building. Baird managed the collection. When Joseph Henry died on May 13, 1878, Spencer Baird took over as secretary.

This mounted African elephant stands in the entrance to the Smithsonian's National Museum of Natural History.

These two men had different ideas about Smithson's purpose. Henry focused on increasing knowledge through research. Baird focused on **diffusing** knowledge by collecting and displaying exhibits. But their two visions came together to represent both aspects of Smithson's purpose.

Adding On

Over the years, new secretaries contributed their own ideas as to what the Smithsonian should be. The institution continued to collect and research. Soon, more buildings and organizations became part of the Smithsonian.

The National Museum of American Art began as private citizen John Varden's personal art collection. Eventually, the collection was transferred to the Smithsonian. The museum grew as more pieces were donated.

Today, the museum holds more than 37,000 items. It displays paintings, sculptures, photographs, drawings, and other pieces of art. Its Renwick Gallery also collects, studies, and displays many examples of American crafts.

The National Air Museum was first established in 1946. When the United States began space exploration, it became the popular National Air and Space Museum. Today, it is an important center for air and space research.

The National Air and Space Museum also holds the world's largest collection of historic aircraft and spacecraft. For example, the plane the Wright brothers flew at Kitty Hawk, North Carolina, in 1903 is on display there. There is even a moon rock visitors can touch!

Smithsonian Buildings on the National Mall in Washington, D.C.

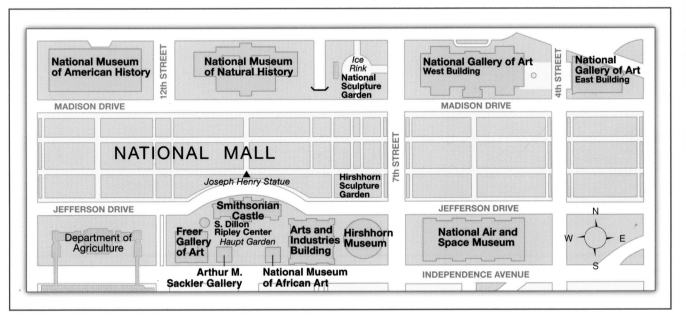

In 1956, Congress saw that the nation needed a museum to house its **cultural** artifacts. Eight years later, the National Museum of History and Technology opened. In 1980, it became the National Museum of American History.

Today, the museum preserves historical and cultural objects as well as oral histories, prints, photographs, and literature. For example, visitors can see the ruby slippers Dorothy wore in the movie *The Wizard of Oz*. Kermit the Frog lives there, too.

These are just a few of the museums included in the Smithsonian Institution. The institution now has 14 museums and a national zoo in Washington, D.C. Two more museums are in New York City. The Smithsonian is also closely **affiliated** with 129 other museums throughout the country.

These giant pandas from China live at the Smithsonian's national zoo. Their names are Mei Xiang and Tian Tian.

Dorothy's ruby slippers from the movie The Wizard of Oz

The Smithsonian's Museums

<u>Washington, D.C.</u>
- Anacostia Museum
- Arts and Industries Building
- Freer and Sackler Galleries
- Hirshhorn Museum and Sculpture Garden
- National Air and Space Museum
- National Museum of African Art
- National Museum of American History, Behring Center
- National Museum of Natural History
- National Portrait Gallery
- National Postal Museum
- National Zoological Park
- Renwick Gallery of the Smithsonian American Art Museum
- Smithsonian American Art Museum
- Smithsonian Institution Building, the Castle

<u>New York City</u>
- Cooper-Hewitt, National Design Museum
- National Museum of the American Indian, George Gustav Heye Center

Children study a statue in one of the Smithsonian's art museums.

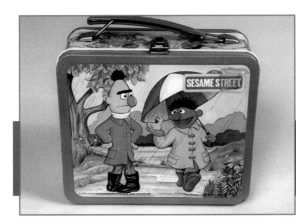

The Smithsonian collects items from American culture, such as this children's lunch box.

The Scientific Side

Today the Smithsonian not only has museums, but still does research, too. For example, scientists study biology at the Tropical Research Institute in Panama. And in Cambridge, Massachusetts, scientists study **astrophysics** at the Smithsonian Astrophysical Observatory.

Another research facility is the Smithsonian Environmental Research Center on Chesapeake Bay in Maryland. There, scientists study the connections between human activities and the environment. Four other centers study birds, ocean life, geology, and other areas of scientific interest.

The Smithsonian publishes much of its research. The Smithsonian Institution Press puts out many scholarly books. *Smithsonian* magazine has articles on science, art, and history. It also includes the results of scientific research projects.

A Smithsonian scientist examines a fossil from a volcano in Maui.

A Man Remembered

In 1904, James Smithson finally made it to the United States. His remains were moved from Genoa, Italy, to Washington, D.C. He was placed in a **crypt** in the Castle. From there, he watches over his creation.

The 1903 Wright Flyer is on display at the National Air and Space Museum in Washington, D.C.

Smithson's legacy still lives on today. The Smithsonian continues to research and preserve scientific and **cultural** items. It also provides educational programs. Scientists around the world make their collections of **specimens**, artifacts, and documents available for study.

Today, Smithson's institution holds nearly 142 million scientific, artistic, and historical objects. Every year, the Smithsonian hosts more than 25 million visitors. Together, research and exhibits work to create the largest museum and research center in the world.

Glossary

affiliate - to associate, as a member, with a person or organization.

architecture - the art of planning and designing buildings. A person who designs architecture is called an architect.

astrophysics - a science that studies stars, planets, and other aspects of space.

asymmetrical - when parts on either side of a centerline are not alike.

cloister - a covered walkway with one side walled and the other side open.

crypt - a room either partially or completely underground, often under a church.

culture - the customs, arts, and tools of a nation or people at a certain time.

debate - to discuss a question or topic, often publicly.

diffusion - the spread of culture or knowledge through contact.

durable - able to exist for a long time without weakening.

meteorology - a science that studies weather and the atmosphere.

regent - a member of a governing board.

specimen - an individual item that is typical of a group.

unconstitutional - something that goes against the laws of a country.

Web Sites

To learn more about the Smithsonian Institution, visit ABDO Publishing Company on the World Wide Web at **www.abdopub.com**. Web sites about the Smithsonian are featured on our Book Links page. These links are routinely monitored and updated to provide the most current information available.

The back of the Castle in Washington, D.C.

Index